blazer BIOS

GOOGLE GLASS
AND
ROBOTICS
INNOVATOR
SEBASTIAN THRUN

MARNE VENTURA

Lerner Publications Company
Minneapolis

Lerner Publications Company
A division of Lerner Publishing Group, Inc.
241 First Avenue North
Minneapolis, MN 55401 U.S.A.

For reading levels and more information, look up this title at www.lernerbooks.com.

Content Consultant: Dr. Arthur C. Sanderson, Professor of Electrical, Computer and Systems Engineering, Rensselaer Polytechnic Institute

Library of Congress Cataloging-in-Publication Data

Ventura, Marne.
    Google Glass and robotics innovator Sebastian Thrun / by Marne Ventura.
       p.   cm. — (STEM trailblazer bios)
    Includes index.
    ISBN 978–1–4677–2459–3 (lib. bdg. : alk. paper)
    ISBN 978–1–4677–2489–0 (eBook)
    1. Thrun, Sebastian, 1967– 2. Robotics—Juvenile literature. 3. Google (Firm)—Juvenile literature. 4. Inventors—Biography—Juvenile literature. I. Title.
TJ211.2.M355 2014
629.8'92092—dc23 [B]   2013026973

Manufactured in the United States of America
1 – PC – 12/31/13

The images in this book are used with the permission of: © Karen Bleier/AFP/Getty Images, p. 4; © Red Line Editorial, p. 5; © Bloomberg/Getty Images, p, 6; © Tomasz Trojanowski/Shutterstock Images, p. 7; © Andrey Yushkov/Shutterstock Images, p. 9; © MTI, Sandor Ujvari/AP Images, p. 10; © Carol M. Highsmith, p. 12; © Kyodo/AP Images, p. 13; © Gene J. Puskar-Pool/Getty Images, p. 14; © DARPA, p. 16; © Gene Blevins/Reuters/Corbis, p. 17; © Karen Bleier/AFP/Getty Images, p. 18; © SuperStock, p. 19; © Eric Risberg/AP Images, p. 20; © Marcio Jose Sanchez/AP Images, p. 22; © Andrew Zarivny/Shutterstock Images, p. 23; © Shutterstock Images, p. 24; © Johannes Simon/Getty Images, p. 25; © Brendan Hoffman/Getty Images, p. 26; © Joe Seer/Shutterstock Images, p. 27.

Front cover: © Udacity

Main body text set in Adrianna Regular 13/22. Typeface provided by Chank.

CONTENTS

Sebastian Thrun works on self-driving cars. He believes they will make people safer.

LEARNING ON
HIS OWN

When Sebastian Thrun was eighteen, he decided that he would someday make cars safer. His best friend had died in a car accident. Thrun wanted to help keep others from the same fate. One of Thrun's most important projects

is his research to develop a self-driving car. Throughout his life, Thrun has used technology to make people's lives better.

EARLY YEARS IN GERMANY

Sebastian Thrun was born in Solingen, Germany, on May 14, 1967. His father was the head of a construction company. His mother was a homemaker. Sebastian was the youngest of three children, but he spent a lot of time alone. When he was eight, he would work on his calculator. He wrote **programs** for games he could play and for solving math problems.

Sebastian grew up and went to college in Germany.

Sebastian has spent his life creating computer programs to make technology better.

Sometimes Sebastian went to a nearby store that sold computers. He would use the store's display computer. But he couldn't save the programs he wrote. He lost all of his **code** every time the computer was turned off. He didn't give up. Sebastian learned to make his programs work with very short coding. That made the code easier to enter the next day.

DRIVEN

Sebastian liked to visit the local arcade. He would drop in a coin and drive a **virtual** car as fast as he could. He had to avoid oil slicks and crazy traffic. When he was twelve, his dad gave him a computer. Sebastian spent hours writing a program to copy the car game from the arcade. It was a big challenge. Sebastian kept working. Finally, he made his own video game.

Sebastian enjoyed a virtual driving game at the arcade so much that he wrote his own video game like it.

Sebastian spent a lot of time working on his computer projects. He also liked to play the piano and sing in a choir. He finished high school with good grades. In college, Sebastian studied computer science, economics, and medicine at the University of Hildesheim in Germany. He worked hard and earned perfect scores on his final exams. He graduated in 1988.

STUDYING ROBOTS

Next, Thrun went to the University of Bonn in Germany. He studied robots and **artificial intelligence (AI)**. He worked with other scientists on a project called Rhino. They made a robot that could learn. Rhino moved around indoors with a camera and a computer built in it. The robot didn't need a human to

TECH TALK

"I always wanted to make robots really smart—so smart that I wouldn't just impress my immediate scientific peers but where they could really help people in society."

—Sebastian Thrun

Thrun studied robots and helped create a robot called Rhino at the University of Bonn in Germany.

run it. Rhino created a map and learned the layout of the room. The robot used sensors to pick up light and movement so it could move around without bumping into walls.

In 1995, Thrun earned an advanced degree in computer science for his research. Scientists at Carnegie Mellon University in Pennsylvania liked Thrun's work. They asked him to come to Pittsburgh. So that year, Thrun moved to the United States.

Chapter 2

Robots are used in factories to make items we use every day, such as cars.

SERVICE ROBOTS

Thrun continued his research at Carnegie Mellon. His goal was to make better **service robots**. In 1997, Thrun and scientists from Germany made Rhino a tour guide. Rhino led tourists around at a museum in Bonn. It knew when people were near. The robot even explained the exhibits to tourists.

MINERVA

By 1998, Thrun and his colleagues (the people he worked with) had built a new robot. They named it Minerva. Minerva had a new feature people liked: a face. The face changed to show the robot's moods. Thrun and his colleagues wanted Minerva to help bridge the gap between robots and people. Minerva interacted with guests and took them on tours of the National Museum of American History in Washington, DC. It rolled up to people and asked them to join the tour. It stopped at displays to share information about them. Guests could clap their hands or touch Minerva's screen to get its attention. The robot also used cameras and the Internet to show the museum to people around the world through a website.

MOODY MINERVA

Minerva was quite moody! The robot interacted with museum visitors and could even speak to them. It could show signs it was happy, such as singing or smiling. If Minerva's path was blocked, its face could frown to show it was upset. Sometimes Minerva even honked its horn at people to let them know they were in the way!

At the National Museum of American History, guests could join Minerva's tours and learn about displays.

NURSEBOT

Next, Thrun mixed what he learned about medicine in college with his knowledge about robots and AI. His goal was to make a robot that could help older people. He started the Nursebot Project. Nursebot reminded people to take their medicine, drink enough water, or go to the doctor. It could sound an alarm in case of an emergency. It used the Internet and a webcam so doctors could see and talk to their patients at home. Nursebot could open the refrigerator door and use the microwave. It could even do laundry for people. It made people feel as if they were not alone.

Nurse robots help people around the world. This nurse robot in Japan can lift people into bed.

A miner is carried up in a capsule and rescued from the July 2002 coal mining accident near Pittsburgh.

GROUNDHOG

In July 2002, there was a coal mining accident near Pittsburgh, Pennsylvania. Nine coal miners were trapped underground after an accident. The maps they used to dig told them they would be safe. But the maps were wrong. The miners dug into an old mine. Water flooded the mine. They could not get out. It took three days to rescue them.

This gave Thrun an idea for a new project. He saw a way for robots to help with accidents such as this in the future. He created Groundhog, a robot that can travel into unsafe mines. Groundhog can find trapped miners and help with their rescue.

TECH TALK

"In the past, robots were . . . predominantly employed on assembly lines and in factory settings. An intelligent service robot like Minerva is a new phenomenon, with implications for health care, janitorial services, surveillance and entertainment. Robots are beginning to make an impact on more than industry and science. They're beginning to make an impact on our everyday lives."

—Sebastian Thrun

Chapter 3

Thrun and his Stanford team created a self-driving car they named Stanley.

A NEW PROJECT

In 2003, Thrun moved from Pennsylvania to California. He taught computer science at Stanford University. In 2004, the US Department of Defense hosted a contest. They asked engineers (people trained to design and build machines) to build a new kind of car. The car had to be able to drive itself across 132 miles (212 kilometers) of desert to win. None of the cars in the contest could do it. Thrun was stunned. He was inspired to create a car that could.

STANLEY THE SELF-DRIVING CAR

Thrun knew he could make a self-driving car for the next contest in 2005. He was then head of the AI lab at Stanford. He put together a team, and Volkswagen gave him three cars to work with. The team worked for many months. They turned a car into a robot by adding cameras, lasers, and **radar**. Thrun and his team named the car Stanley after Stanford.

Early on the morning of October 8, 2005, teams got ready to race their vehicles in the Mojave Desert in Nevada. There were twenty-three vehicles in the race. The team to finish the fastest would win. Stanley won the contest! The prize of $2 million went to Stanford.

Thrun and his team celebrate Stanley's win.

A Google Street View vehicle takes pictures while driving around Virginia.

GOOGLE STREET VIEW

In 2007, Thrun and four of his students came up with a new project to gather information. They mounted cameras onto cars. Then the cars were driven all over the world. The cameras took photos of buildings. Thrun and his students entered the photos and addresses of the buildings into a huge collection of data called a database. The photos and addresses were organized and easy to search in the database. Anyone could go online and look at photos of almost any place in the world.

Thrun began to work with engineers from Google. His photo-mapping project became Google Street View. With Google Street View, viewers can explore different places around the world as if they're actually there. They can take a virtual tour of their favorite landmark. They can even venture into a restaurant to see what it looks like.

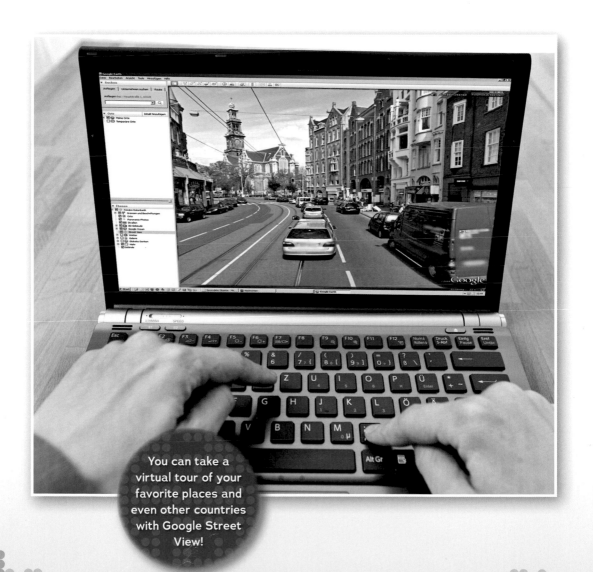

You can take a virtual tour of your favorite places and even other countries with Google Street View!

Thrun continues to work on technology to make self-driving cars safe for people to drive every day.

SELF-DRIVING CAR

In 2010, Thrun announced that he was working on another self-driving car. He wants to create a car that works anywhere—not just in the open desert. Thrun has developed

TECH TALK

"As a boy, I loved cars. When I turned 18, I lost my best friend to a car accident . . . And then I decided I would dedicate my life to saving one million people every year . . . Our [self-driving] cars have sensors with which they magically can see everything around them and make decisions about every aspect of driving. It's the perfect driving mechanism."

—*Sebastian Thrun*

ways to make a group of Google's cars drive safely on their own. The cars have built-in computers to guide them. They use both stored and online maps to find their way. They have sensors to see everything around them. They can drive safely in heavy city traffic or on winding mountain roads. The sensors let them know if something is in the way, and they can even drive when it is dark out.

Thrun believes self-driving cars will make people safer when they drive. The computers and sensors in the cars could help prevent accidents. He also thinks these self-driving cars will make it easier to get from place to place. Elderly or disabled

Children look inside a self-driving car at Google headquarters in California.

people could use these cars to get around. Self-driving cars could save people time too. The average worker in the United States spends fifty-two minutes each day driving to and from work. This time could be spent doing something else.

Thrun's cars have been tested on more than 140,000 miles (225,308 kilometers) of road. They always have a human driver who can take control if something goes wrong. But so far, the self-driving cars have not failed.

Thrun's self-driving cars have even been able to drive themselves down the eight curvy turns on Lombard Street in San Francisco, California!

DO NOT ENTER

Teaching at Stanford University gave Thrun an idea to improve the way people can earn an education.

USING TECHNOLOGY TO TEACH

Thrun taught classes at Stanford from 2003 to 2011. He saw the need for a change in education. He wanted people to be able to continue their education their whole lives—not just for a few years after high school. He also felt that money, work, busy schedules, or distance from a college shouldn't keep anyone from getting an education.

Thrun worked with Peter Norvig, an AI expert at Google. Together they decided to offer the AI class Thrun was teaching at Stanford in a new way: online. People could take it over the Internet for free. Thrun sent out an e-mail to announce it, and 160,000 students signed up.

Thrun speaks at a conference about his ideas for improving education.

Thrun accepts the American Ingenuity Award from *Smithsonian Magazine* in 2012 for creating Udacity.

UDACITY

Thrun designed a website for the class. Students from around the world visited the class online when they had time. Instead of a long lecture and a single test, students watched lots of short videos. There was a quick quiz at the end of each video. Students could watch the videos and take the quizzes over and over again until they passed. They could move at their own pace.

Thrun was happy about the success of the class. Soldiers, working single moms, and the sick were able to learn when they had time. In 2012, Thrun decided to start a new website for online education. He called it Udacity. Students around the world can take Udacity classes for free.

GOOGLE GLASS

In 2012, Thrun and a team of researchers began developing Google Glass. They want to explore how a computer can be worn like a pair of eyeglasses. This hands-free device rests on your ears but does not cover your eyes. You look up to see the glass. It has a built-in computer as well as a microphone and a camera.

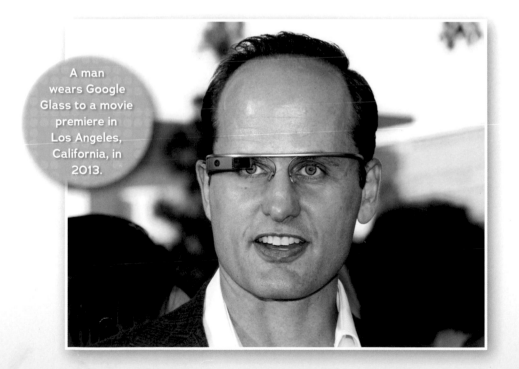

A man wears Google Glass to a movie premiere in Los Angeles, California, in 2013.

Your voice tells Google Glass what to do. You can tell it to snap a photo of what you are looking at. If you say, "Record a video," it records what you are watching. Someone else can watch the video over the Internet at the same time you are seeing it. You can ask questions or ask for directions. Glass searches for answers on the Internet. You can even ask how to say something in a different language. Thrun and the Google Glass team hope the project will make it easier for people to use technology.

Science and technology have always been a big part of Thrun's life. His ideas and inventions are already helping make life better for people. What wild idea will he develop next?

TECH TALK

"The key for being innovative is to admit that we don't know and that we have to learn. . . . Every human being is made to learn. I believe in every single kid in every single school."

—*Sebastian Thrun*

TIMELINE

1967

Sebastian Thrun is born in Solingen, Germany, on May 14.

1988

Thrun graduates from the University of Hildesheim in Germany with degrees in computer science, economics, and medicine.

1995

Thrun moves to the United States. He works as a research computer scientist at Carnegie Mellon University.

2003

Thrun moves to California and teaches computer science at Stanford University.

2005

Thrun and his team from Stanford create a self-driving car named Stanley.

2007

Thrun launches Google Street View.

2010

Thrun becomes a fellow, or researcher, for Google. He also announces his work on a new self-driving car.

2012

Thrun founds Udacity. He and a team of researchers begin developing Google Glass.

2013

A test version of Glass is released to several thousand "explorers."

GLOSSARY

artificial intelligence (AI)
the power of a machine to copy human behavior, or the field of science studying this

code
a set of instructions for a computer program

programs
step-by-step instructions that tell a computer to do something with data

radar
a device that sends out radio waves to detect and locate surrounding objects

service robots
robots that provide a service to humans

virtual
existing on a computer or online

SOURCE NOTES

8   Jason Williams, "The Innovators Who Are Rocking the World," January 16, 2013, http://centricindy.org/the-innovators-who-are-rocking-the-world.

15 Heather Bruce, "Minerva, the Robotic Tour Guide," Lemelson Center, accessed July 20, 2013, http://invention.smithsonian.org/resources/online_articles_detail.aspx?id=356.

21 Sebastian Thrun, "Sebastian Thrun: Google's Driverless Car," *Huffington Post*, accessed July 21, 2013, http://www.huffingtonpost.com/2011/12/06/self-driving-car_n_1130568.html.

28 Sebastian Thrun, "Sebastian Thrun on the Future of Learning," Smithsonian Media, accessed July 21, 2013, http://www.smithsonianmag.com/video/Sebastian-Thrun-on-the-Future-of-Learning.html.

FURTHER INFORMATION

BOOKS

Brasch, Nicolas. *Robots of the Future*. New York: PowerKids Press, 2013. Learn how robots are already a part of everyday life and what the future might hold for robots and people.

Chaffee, Joel. *How to Build a Prize-Winning Robot*. New York: Rosen, 2011. Want to create your own robot and beat the competition? Check out this book.

Kaplan, Arie. *The Awesome Inner Workings of Video Games*. Minneapolis: Lerner Publications, 2014. Find out what's inside your favorite games and gaming system and how it all works.

WEBSITES

NASA Space Place: Robots
http://spaceplace.nasa.gov/stereo-vision/en
Read about how some robots are built to see like humans.

Smithsonian: Ocean Portal
http://ocean.si.edu/ocean-news/underwater-robots-explore-ocean
Learn how underwater robots are used to explore the oceans.

Smithsonian: The Lemelson Center
http://invention.smithsonian.org/resources/online_articles_detail.aspx?id=356
Read more about the service robot Minerva.

INDEX

ABOUT THE AUTHOR

Marne Ventura is a former elementary school teacher who writes educational material for children in kindergarten to sixth grade. She has helped create more than fifty software products and apps for math, science, reading, and social studies. Ventura lives with her husband on the central coast of California.